REINCARNATION

Slipping In and Out of the Flesh

D1291544

REINCARNATION

Slipping In and Out of the Flesh

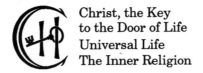

Christ, the Key
to the Door of Life
Universal Life
The Inner Religion

2nd Edition 1996

Published by:
© Universal Life
The Inner Religion
PO Box 3549
Woodbridge, CT 06525
U S A

Licensed edition
translated from the original German title:
"Reincarnation
Das Heraus- und Hineinschlüpfen in das Fleisch"

From the Universal Life Series
with the consent of
© Verlag DAS WORT GmbH
im Universellen Leben
Max-Braun-Strasse 2
97828 Marktheidenfeld/Altfeld
Germany

Order No. S 420en

The German edition is the work of reference for all
questions regarding the meaning of the contents

ISBN 3-89201-085-4

"Say, what has fate in store for us?
Say, how did it connect us
so precisely?
Ah, you were in lifetimes past
my sister or my wife."

Johann Wolfgang von Goethe

Table of Contents

I. The Relevance of Knowledge about Reincarnation at the Beginning of the Age of Aquarius

Today, in a time of spiritual awakening, at the beginning of the Age of Aquarius, a basic question, and at the same time an age-old adage of mankind, is a subject of increasing relevance: the knowledge about reincarnation, that is, the possibility a soul has to incarnate several times in a human body. The teaching of reincarnation is part of early Christian thought—even though the Church erased it from western thought. It gives answers to questions concerning suffering and death, the purpose of life on earth, and about life after this life. As a part-aspect of the law of cause and effect, reincarnation offers a chance for the intensive purification of the soul.

The following explanations, which throw light on the subject of reincarnation from an original Christian point of view, present in detail the spiritual principles that pertain to reincarnation. They are based on the knowledge revealed by the Spirit of God which is taught in Universal Life, an Original Christian community of the present times.

Reincarnation—a basic question and an age-old adage of mankind

Reincarnation—this is a basic adage of mankind. At all times and in most cultures this subject has been an element of faith and of speculation. The well-known Swiss psychologist C. G. Jung held that: "Reincarnation is an expression which definitely belongs to the age-old statements of mankind. These age-old adages are based on what I call the 'archetype.' In their very origin all statements regarding the supernatural are determined by the archetype, so that it is not surprising that we find statements about reincarnation among many peoples." [1]

Knowledge about the reincarnation of a soul is the basis for a satisfactory interpretation of suffering and guilt—of the very meaning of existence. It gives an answer to the question why children are born in misery, crippled and sick. From the religious point of view, the same question is raised: How is this possible if a God of love exists? On the other hand, why are many people born into wealth, prosperity and health? And, why are there so-called child prodigies?

The question of whether there is a possibility of repeated lives on earth is a most essential one. It concerns the very basic interpretation of our human existence; it relates to concepts of man, of the world, and of God.

Knowledge about reincarnation is not only widespread in eastern religions—for example, Hinduism and Buddhism—but to many great western poets and thinkers of bygone and modern times, this knowledge is self-evident to their way of thinking. Empedocles, Pythagoras, Plato and Virgil, and then later Goethe, Hölderlin, Schiller, Schleiermacher, Fichte, Kant, Schopenhauer, Nietzsche, Kierkegaard and Voltaire, among others, were convinced of the possibility of repeated lives on earth.

Today the idea of reincarnation is upheld by large esoteric movements, for example, the Anthroposophists, the Rosicrucians or the Lorber groups. Universal Life, too, upholds the teaching of the possibility of several incarnations in a human body for a soul.

Science, too, is interested in reincarnation. Extensive material is available, for example, the work of Prof. Jan Stevenson who, after several years of research on over 1,500 cases of spontaneous recollection, expressed the conviction that the cases scientifically examined by him "by far exceed the mere suggestion of reincarnation; to me they adequately prove it."

Another well-known name is Thorwald Dethlefsen who led his patients back into former lives by means of a method which he himself developed, thus bringing to light memories deeply rooted in the soul. He used this method to treat psychosomatic ailments in their present life.[2]

Despite, or rather because of, these research results and the widespread knowledge about reincarnation, there is no standard doctrine but many different opinions which of course overlap, and in part coincide, in their essence and in the application of this knowledge.

It is like the question about God: All religions affirm His existence—but there are different concepts about His nature. Everywhere there are smaller or larger sparks of the one truth, mixed with differing human opinions and conceptions. The same applies to reincarnation. The fact is hardly denied, but when it comes to the details the statements can differ considerably. For instance, the concept of reincarnation cannot simply be identified with the transmigration of the soul; eastern understanding differs from western—depending on which image of God it is based upon.

Unlike the opinion of the Catholic and Protestant teachings, we are convinced that there is also a Christian viewpoint on the doctrine of reincarnation and, moreover, that the knowledge about the reincarnation of the soul is part of early Christian thought and an essential element of Christian faith.

"The knowledge about reincarnation was a fixed part of Christian thought during the time of early Christianity and its first centuries. Jesus of Nazareth also taught about reincarnation and many church scholars considered reincarnation as self-evident." [3]

Hermann Bauer confirmed this in his work on reincarnation.[4] He critically evaluated Greek and Latin biblical texts, council documents and works of early church fathers, and came to the conclusion that reincarnation is an early Christian teaching. References in the Bible are, for example, found in Matthew 16:14 (also Luke 9:19), when Jesus asked who people thought He was. Thereupon His disciples answered Him that some thought Him to be John the Baptist, others Elijah, and yet others Jeremia or some other prophet. In another example, Jesus spoke of the return of Elijah, meaning John the Baptist (Mt. 17:10-13; also Luke 9:8 and others).

The church teacher Rufinus confirmed in a letter to Anastasius that the belief in repeated lives was common knowledge for the church fathers and that, at all times, it had been passed on as an old tradition. Origenes (ca. 185-254), who was one of the greatest Greek church fathers, taught reincarnation with strong conviction; the original Bible manuscripts in Greek and Hebrew were still at his disposal.[5]

The doctrine of reincarnation was thus a constituent part of Christianity in the first centuries. All the more surprising, that this knowledge was and is not taught by western churches.

Church versus reincarnation

How did the elimination of the truth about reincarnation develop? Let us look into this question briefly.

For many reasons, both political and human, numerous theological disputes about the teachings of Origenes broke out. Since Origenes was acknowledged everywhere as a prominent figure in the early church—he was the authority, and both opponents as well as supporters referred to him—knowledge about reincarnation became more and more associated with his name. In the course of the following centuries, the dispute about Origenes became increasingly strong, thus requiring a definitive decision. And so, a crucial event followed which resulted in the repression and elimination of the doctrine of reincarnation: At the synod of the Orthodox Church in the year 543 in Constantinople, the teachings of Origines were banned with nine anathemas (curses).

Among them were two curses which indirectly condemned the teaching of reincarnation. First, the pre-existence of the soul is denied and, in this connection, that souls originally existed as pure beings in heaven who then, however, broke away from God and incarnated into human bodies. Secondly, all those are cursed who do not believe there is an eternal damnation for demons and impious men as well as punishment for all those who believe in a reintegration return to God (apocatastasis).[6]

The formulation of these anathemas was carried out per the instructions of Emperor Justinian I who considered himself the supreme ruler of the church. The anathemas ordered by him were confirmed by the synod of 543 and, ten years later, Pope Vigilius signed the curses submitted to him by the Council of Constantinople, although according to council reports they had not been discussed at all.

The personality of Emperor Justinian, the general conditions of war in the Eastern Roman Empire, and the threatening danger of being confronted with an additional internal political-religious front in Palestine were the political motives for the elimination of the doctrine of reincarnation.

In order to fill the gap resulting from the condemnation of the teaching of reincarnation and in order to support the doctrine of only one human life, new dogmas had to be created. These dealt mainly with original sin, creation of the soul at the moment of begetting, mortal sin, judgment day, purgatory and eternal damnation. At the same time, the necessity of salvation through priestly intermediaries was established, for without them this system of doctrines could not have functioned.

With this however, the questions about the meaning of suffering and guilt that were stated at the beginning are, from the very start, unanswerable. With empty theological phrases, people who ask existential questions are consoled with the apparent mysteries of God which should not be put into question.[7]

II. Origin, Nature and Spiritual Aim of Man

The possibility of repeated lives on earth of one and the same soul is a basic truth of our human existence. In order to understand the meaning and significance of this, we should first become aware of the origin, nature and spiritual aim of man.

The Fall of the angels

Originally, we human beings were pure angels, divine beings from the eternal heavens. We are children of God, perfect images of God-Father, who once lived in the seven dimensional Absoluteness, in the light of God. We cannot imagine the glorious heavenly life of these pure spirit beings; we can at best have a sense of it in moments of highest inner bliss. It is a life of being directly permeated by the Spirit of God, by God's radiating light, a life of infinite fullness, joy, harmony and love.[8]

However, one spirit being, Satana, turned away from God; she had negative sensations and began to imagine a kingdom of her own.

Here, in the willfulness of Satana, lies the origin of the so-called Fall-event, also called "Fall of the angels."[9]

Satana enticed other spirit beings into disobedience towards God; as a result of their unlawful behavior—they violated the divine law of love through their willful actions—they were increasingly incapable of being irradiated by the spirit of God; their light visibly decreased. When they did not listen to the instructions of the cherubim (archangels) either, they were led from the pure heavens by the archangel, Michael.

As a result of the departure of these disloyal children of God, the so-called wall of light developed, which encloses the pure heavens. The more a spirit being turns away from God through its negative, that is, egotistic and willful, actions, the more energy it gives to this wall of the law.

Because the fall beings continuously violated the law, a steadily increasing condensation of the once fine-material forms took place. This happened to the formerly pure spirit beings as well as to parts of the spiritual planets that had left the pure heavens with them. In this way, little by little and according to their degree of condensation, the seven so-called Fall-planes with their seven respective sub-levels developed.

The energy potential of the ether bodies belonging to the once light-filled spirit beings reduced more and more; they became dark and shadowed. The ether body became smaller and smaller, and seven times seven garments developed around it. In their vibrations, these garments are identical with the Fall-planes. We call this shadowed, covered body, the soul.

The soul is the book of life. All sensations, thoughts, words and actions, whether positive or negative, are recorded in it. The negative vibrations constitute the shadowing (the burden) of the soul. They are the garments, or veils of clouds, which keep away the divine light.

Because of this increasing condensation, the soul became encapsulated more and more. The seven garments, also called soul garments, drew together into spiritually compressed points which are called consciousness centers (chakras). Via these consciousness centers the formation of the coarse-material body ensued and man came into being. The human body is, so to speak, the vehicle of the soul, with which it moves in matter—which in the meantime had also developed.

The deed of redemption of Jesus, the Christ

As a result of the life of the fall beings that was adverse to God, the spiritual atoms, of which their ether bodies consist, rotated more and more slowly, leading to the aforementioned condensation. Satana, who was now also called Lucifer (light bearer), planned to make the spiritual atoms rotate so slowly that they would reverse their direction from right to left. This would have meant a successive degeneration finally leading to the dissolution of all forms into the eternal ether. This concept of the dissolution of all forms is still an element in eastern religions, all of which were founded before Christ.

However, Jesus, the Christ, the incarnated Son of God, stopped this process with His deed of redemption.[10] When He said on Golgotha: "It is finished," His divine heritage divided into sparks and a so-called Redeemer-spark became embedded in each soul, in each human being. This is active as the Christ-force in the fourth consciousness center, a supporting and maintaining energy that upholds the divine filiation of God in each soul, thus preventing further degeneration. The Christ-spark is the redeeming and healing power within us.

It was also the mission of Jesus, the Christ, to teach the path back to Absoluteness to a mankind which had gone astray, for many prophets before Him had tried this in vain. He, the greatest prophet and mystic in the history of mankind, proclaimed the path of selfless love, the path within. In the Sermon on the Mount, His teaching is summarized in a concentrated form; it is an offer proffered by God, who wants to lead His children back to the eternal home, to the heavens of light.

By way of the deed of redemption of Jesus Christ, each one of us bears the Redeemer-spark within himself, and this spark strives to return into the Absoluteness, into the

Kingdom of God. It is a force that presses for self-recognition, for change—from an externalized life that is oriented towards wanting to possess, to be and to have. It is the transforming and redeeming flame in every heart, the guiding light for each one who seriously turns to Christ and to the divine laws.

The aim of soul and person

And so, the goal of every soul and of every person is—whether this is accepted or not—to become again a conscious child of God, a free heavenly being which lives and acts in the light of God, sharing His power and glory.

To accomplish this, it is necessary to lighten the seven soul garments which are active as consciousness centers within the human being and to make the energy body—the once pure spirit body that has been shadowed and darkened by an unlawful life—shine again until it is uncovered once more and can be completely irradiated by the Spirit of God. For, we are of divine origin.

The meaning of life on earth—
the earth as a school of life

The above-mentioned path back to the Absoluteness, the metamorphosis from man to God-man, to a conscious child of light, can be walked as a discarnate soul in the seven Fall-planes—which since the Redeemer-deed of Jesus, the Christ, are also called planes of purification and preparation—as well as in the human garment. It is the path of the step-by-step purification of the soul from all burdens, the path of selfless love that leads back to the heart of God.

On earth we have the possibility to complete all seven consciousness levels with their sub-levels, to dissolve all consciousness centers. In this way, the earth is also a place of grace, a school of life, in which we can purify ourselves considerably faster than in the planes of purification. The reason for this will be explained later.

And so, the time on earth is precious and should be a time of growing awareness, a time of intensive effort to purify the soul and to spiritualize the person, by recognizing and overcoming one's faults and burdens and by a life of selfless love.

III. Karma and reincarnation on the path to perfection

The law of cause and effect

In the four lower Fall-planes—matter with earth being the lowest—the law of cause and effect, also called causal law or law of sowing and reaping, is in force. It says, you will reap what you sow!

The sum of the negative causes that we have set and have not yet expiated is our soul burden, also called karma. The law of cause and effect means: Whatever bad we have sown, every negative cause, every cause which opposes the divine law of life and of love, tends towards producing its effect one day.

The soul burden is brought to a head under the irradiation of the planets according to immutable laws. Once ripe, it is set in motion in the soul through a corresponding planetary constellation and can then flow out of the human being via its body.

The soul burden can pour into the body in the form of illness or blows of fate; it can appear as pain, worries, problems and difficulties with one's fellow men, with one's life-partner or children. We must and may make amends for the things we once caused.

This may not happen until centuries later in another incarnation, depending on the planetary constellation and other conditions which we will address later. So this is the reason why children are born crippled. Through their illness, they expiate causes which they had set in an earlier life.

Uninformed people cannot understand this seemingly senseless affliction. They either submit without thinking about it, or they refer to the mysteries of God, or they blame God. In their spiritual blindness, they think that He sends hardship and illness. They do not know that God, the infinite love, never punishes nor sends any kind of suffering. He simply allows the effects of the causes created by the person himself, so that he may recognize himself through this and turn back.

In this way, the free will of man is upheld. We ourselves determine our fate. Everything that happens to us is the effect of causes that we ourselves have created. So we have joy and sorrow in our own hands—as we sow, will we reap.

The law of correspondence

We already mentioned that the earth is a school of life which, though resulting from the Fall-event, is also a gift of grace from our heavenly Father. This means that the soul can purify itself here more quickly than in the spheres of purification of the beyond, when the person has died and has put aside his material body.

When a person puts aside his body, his soul is attracted by that sphere of the beyond which corresponds to his vibration, to his state of consciousness. There, he meets souls which have a similar consciousness and resemble him in some aspects.

But on earth we meet people of the most differing consciousness, and with all kinds of faults and weaknesses. Because of this, we have the chance to recognize our own negative character traits much easier here, if we apply the law of correspondence. This law states that whatever disturbs or irritates me about my neighbor also lies in me.

When a certain peculiarity of my neighbor irritates me, this means that the same or something similar lies in me. Just as the vibrating string of a violin can make the same string of another violin vibrate, in the same way a soul burden starts to vibrate in our soul, a so-called correspondence, if another person behaves in a corresponding way. And so, our neighbor is our mirror who can help us recognize ourselves—if we only look into it.

The law of forgiveness and grace

If the law of cause and effect were to hold without limitation, we would have to expiate and suffer through every negative cause created by us.

However, by the grace of God we have the possibility to escape this severe fate. Namely, if we recognize our faulty behavior in time and repent of it sincerely, if we ask for forgiveness and, as far as possible, make amends for what we have caused, then the guilt can be expiated in a less severe form or even dissolved. This is in the will of God; it will happen in a way that is good for the development of our soul.

But here, too, the forgiveness of the person who was harmed plays an essential role. As long as everything has not been cleared between our neighbor and ourselves, we remain bound to our guilt and also to him, thereby hindering our spiritual development as well as his.

The more we open ourselves to the power of God that lies within us through a righteous life, an increasingly selfless life, the more He can grant us His grace. When Christ walked in the earthly garment as the Son of God, He said: "Come unto Me, all of you who are weary and heavy laden. I will give you rest." (Mt. 11:28)

At any time we can turn to Christ, whose redeeming Spirit, the Redeemer-spark, lies within us. We can deliver everything into His hands; for He wants to carry our burdens with us and relieve us of them wholly or partly, just as it is good for our soul.

The teaching of reincarnation
in the original Christian sense

If life on earth offers the possibility for a soul to purify itself here more quickly than in the spheres of the beyond (the purification planes), then repeated incarnations are a chance to make amends more quickly.

However, this means that the incarnation into a human body corresponds to the will of God only when the soul is prepared to accept earth as a school of life and as a place to expiate the causes that it itself has created. So it is not the will of God that a person, bound to the fate that he himself has created, incarnates again and again.

The spiritual law of gravitation

Before we speak about the different reasons and possibilities for a soul to incarnate into a human body, we first have to be aware of a spiritual principle, namely the spiritual law of gravitation.[11] It says that like attracts like. This is a spiritual law—not a physical law which applies to magnets, whereby opposite poles attract each other.

The spiritual law of gravitation says that similar vibrations attract each other. For the soul this means that whatever is active within it, whatever vibrates in it, determines its place of destination, whether after death, in the planes of purification, or in a new incarnation.

In order to incarnate into a physical body, a soul requires a certain constellation of spiritual and material planets which corresponds to its radiation tendency. On the other hand, according to the spiritual law of gravitation, the vibrational tendency of an expectant mother has to correspond to the vibration of the incarnating soul.

At the moment of procreation, a soul is called upon by both parents via the bonds of cause and effect. Both husband and wife have a soul burden to expiate with the soul they called, or they have a task to fulfill with it on earth.

As a result of procreation, a so-called radiation band develops and thus, a connection with a soul in the spheres of purification.

At the moment of procreation, a soul hears the call to incarnation and makes contact with the fertilized ovum. In the same way as the cells divide and the development and growth of the embryo take place in the mother's body, the soul approaches the developing body.[12]

Instruction and free will in the purification planes

No soul incarnates without receiving an explanation; every soul is instructed before its incarnation. So-called teaching angels draw the soul's attention to what lies ahead during its life on earth. It is also enlightened about the spiritual laws which apply to matter, for example, the law of cause and effect.

Many souls are even advised against a further incarnation for the time being; this happens when the teaching angels see, from the composition of the soul, that an incarnation at this time could entail even greater burdens for the soul.

A further incarnation is recommended to some souls, particularly when the soul shows a certain degree of maturity and is willing to develop even faster through an incarnation, thus drawing nearer to God and its true eternal being.

But every soul is given free will. If a soul wants to incarnate, it can do so on the condition that a suitable planetary constellation exists and that it is attracted by a certain soul composition of an expectant mother—the father is also playing a certain role in this.

The souls can also continue their development in the planes of purification. They are guided individually by the teaching angels. Since the soul in the spheres beyond has lost its sense of time and space, it can take centuries or millennia until it listens to reason and considers further development—another reason why development on earth can be much faster than in the planes of purification.

If a soul has been living for a very long time on one and the same spiritual purification planet in the beyond, the following happens:[13] The Christ-force which had enveloped the soul thus far withdraws, thus exposing the soul to a more intensive influence of cosmic forces. Gradually, these penetrate more and more strongly, reflecting in the soul stored images of former misdeeds which it committed while in the human body. The struggle then begins in the soul. It defends itself against the rising pictures, thus fighting against its own deeds.[14]

Through this cosmic radiation the soul is pushed to a decision. Either it strives towards further development in the spheres of purification or through a new incarnation in the school of earth.

Without this pushing of the Spirit and as a consequence of its lack of a sense of time, many a soul would remain at the same level of development for a very long time. They would not even realize that they are stagnating and thus would not strive to continue in their development.

Here too, free will is respected; for in the Spirit there is no must—not even regarding incarnation. The soul is only encouraged, not forced, to reach a decision; for the pushing of the Spirit must be understood as a helping hand so that the soul does not remain on the same level of development—which is not possible in the long run—but goes on growing into the consciousness of God.

Reasons and possibilities for incarnation

And so, the souls are instructed in the spheres of the beyond, also regarding the laws for a new incarnation and the possible consequences of an incarnation. We have already mentioned that it is not the will of God that souls go into the flesh again and again without accepting the earth as a school of life.

But since each soul has free will, many choose the path of incarnation, ignoring the will of God. These are egocentric souls tightly bound to matter who believe that the material world with its pleasures and passions is the only reality. For these heavily burdened souls, only the sensual life is important. They do not want to know anything about God and His love or about a higher spiritual development.

According to the spiritual law of like attracts like, these souls are mostly born into suffering and infirmity, provided that the above-mentioned conditions (planetary constellation, corresponding vibrational tendency of the parents) are fulfilled. This is also one of the reasons why so many souls incarnate in developing countries at the present time; their state of consciousness corresponds to the spiritual and physical conditions prevalent in these countries.

However, we should not deduce from these facts that all people born into affliction and suffering in developing countries are heavily burdened souls.

Besides these driven souls, this group of heavily-burdened souls which incarnate like sleep-walkers, so to speak—unconcerned about where the wheel of reincarnation draws them and not caring whether they are born disabled or whether they are destined for only a short earthly life—there are also those which are heavily burdened, but take the step towards incarnation deliberately. In the brevity of space and time, they wish to expiate the soul burden that they have recognized and to suffer through what they could otherwise expiate only during very long periods of time in the soul realms.

A third group of souls incarnate in the so-called Third World in order to help their brothers and sisters, to serve them with selfless love, and, at the same time, to pay off their own recognized burden.[15]

Additionally, many of them come to earth with a divine mission engraved in their souls in order to live God's love as an example for mankind and to proclaim it to them. They want to bring light into the darkness of matter and to teach people the spiritual laws.

Birth control and overpopulation

In the so-called civilized parts of the world, many heavily burdened souls also press for incarnation. They stimulate in man the need for culinary pleasures, for alcohol or drugs. Such excesses promote a sexual life which provides these souls, in turn, with the possibility of incarnating into this world.

However, because of abortion, birth control and other contraceptive methods, many souls striving towards incarnation in the West no longer have the possibility to incarnate. This is a further spiritual reason for the population explosion in the Third World. This means that when birth control is successful in one country, there will be a greater number of incarnations in another country or in the poor areas of other countries. If incarnations are hindered in one part of the world, there will be an overpopulation in another region in its stead.

One could compare overpopulation with a disease that is stopped in the body with medicines and thus pushed back in the soul. In this way, further causes are created, which may come up in other organs with completely different symptoms. Whatever has not been completely worked out seeks side channels again and again. What has been merely postponed is far from being resolved.

Knowledge is covered over—Risk and chance

When living in a material body, a person no longer remembers the spiritual knowledge that the soul had before incarnation. Neither does he know of his former lives on earth. This means that upon each incarnation the knowledge about former lives and the sojourn in the spheres beyond is covered. This is why each soul runs the risk of burdening itself during its life on earth, no matter how pure it may be.

This also happened to many messengers of light sent by God in order to teach mankind His love. They became entangled in matter; they were caught by the wheel of cause and effect and then often had to expiate, during several earthly lives, the karma that they themselves had built up, and to dissolve it in a life according to the divine laws.

Nevertheless, covering up its previous knowledge during the incarnation of the soul in a human body is not only a risk, but also a great chance when compared to the life of the soul in the worlds beyond. Such knowledge would be a tremendous burden; we would torture ourselves with reproaches, just like the souls in the planes of purification. We would be hindered from living in the present and would be unable to perceive and use the present possibilities for self-recognition and making amends, without being influenced by the results of our former wrongdoing. Therefore, it would take much longer and be more difficult to progress in our spiritual development.

Every day, even every hour and every minute on earth, offers the possibility for self-recognition and clearing up our soul burdens, if we are open, clear and aware. Whatever comes towards us does not occur by chance, but happens to us according to immutable laws; it is the fruit of our once sown seed.

In light of this background knowledge, it becomes clear that the deliberate uncovering of former incarnations by means of certain techniques, for whatever motive, is not law-abiding; it interferes in the predetermined process of maturation of a soul debt. One's vision is focused on the past instead of perceiving the present possibilities for self-recognition.

Liberation from the wheel of reincarnation

The mystical path of love

Seen from a spiritual point of view, the meaning and purpose of life on earth—and thus of repeated incarnations of the soul into a material body—is to purify the soul garments and thus ascend towards God step-by-step; it is the successive unfoldment of the originally pure and fine spirit body.

The quickest way to reach this goal is to walk the so-called Inner Path consciously, the path to the inner sanctum, which all true mystics have walked, are walking and will walk—for every person is the temple of God and the Spirit of God is within him. The Inner Path consists of recognizing oneself and discarding all human, egotistical attitudes and faults step-by-step. This path is also the path of the unfoldment of selfless love.

The Original Christians in Universal Life consciously strive for and live this process, which leads to the successive dissolution of the consciousness centers and their respective soul garments, that is, soul burdens. They walk the Christian mystical path of love, which is taught in the Christian Mystery School. With the Christ-force they walk the path of self-recognition and actualization of the divine laws—all the way to their fulfillment.

Rebirth in the Spirit

The aim of the school of earth that man grow out of the law of cause and effect, through the purification of soul and person, and into the Absolute Law. As soon as the first four consciousness levels are opened, the impersonal selfless love acts powerfully. Then the Christ-force is also fully active; through the so-called inner word or the purified sensations, Christ can lead us back directly to the absolute consciousness.

As soon as the fourth level—which also corresponds to the fourth level of the purification planes in the worlds beyond—has been opened, the person, that is, the soul, is no longer subject to the causal law; the so-called wheel of reincarnation has been left behind. The soul no longer has to incarnate in order to expiate its burden and is no longer under the influence of the planets. It has reached its first large goal on the path back to God, the so-called rebirth in the Spirit.

This is the return into the law of God for the most part. In the three so-called planes of preparation, the soul can then completely purify itself. However, only the soul which has accepted Christ as its Redeemer, as the first-beheld Son of God and Co-regent of infinity can walk through the wall of light surrounding the heavenly worlds. It brings the Redeemer-spark, which has become a bright flame in it, back into the Absoluteness.

IV. Consequences

The concept of God, of the world and of man in light of the doctrine of reincarnation

From what we have stated it follows quite clearly that the acceptance of the doctrine of reincarnation is of great importance in explaining the meaning of human existence. Questions regarding guilt, suffering and liberation, which otherwise can hardly or only inadequately be answered, thus find a plausible answer. A full understanding of human reality and of life in the beyond is made possible. Man is tied into the great cosmic events that are determined by immutable spiritual laws, and yet in his innermost being he is an absolutely free, light-filled, pure, divine being. Even as a shadowed soul, he always has free will.

In light of the doctrine of reincarnation, the God of love also becomes more clearly visible—without the theological constriction stating that God chastises those whom He loves. He is and remains the love; He does not send suffering or disease to anyone; He does not cast any soul into a crippled human body for some mysterious reason or other, and He does not make of anyone a child prodigy. The way a person will be born as a human being is determined by himself alone.

Our heavenly Father has given us free will. Therefore, we are also responsible for what we do and don't do. It is a given that we have to harvest the seed which we ourselves have sown in former lives—if we do not change our ways. It is not God who punishes us but we ourselves. He only allows the effects of the causes which we ourselves have set.

And so, in this light the earth and a human life do not appear to be a damnation nor a last destination. Even though the earth has come into existence in its material form through the Fall-event, it is also offered to us by God as a school of life, as a possibility and chance to purify ourselves quickly from our soul burden—which could last eons in the beyond.

From an original Christian point of view, the doctrine of reincarnation also states that there can be no eternal damnation. Heaven and hell are within us; they are conditions of consciousness. Since every soul bears in itself the Redeemer-spark which strives to return to the Absoluteness again, it will continue to develop more or less quickly; sooner or later each soul will return to the pure heavens.

This also means that there is no retrogression nor degeneration of the soul. Through the Redeemer-spark, the filiation of God is maintained within the soul, however burdened it may be. This means that to reincarnate as an animal or even as a plant ("transmigration of the soul") is not possible. The eastern religions teach this because their scripts came into existence before the Redeemer-deed of Jesus Christ and therefore do not contain the knowledge of the sacrifice on Golgotha, which once and for all, stopped the degeneration and dissolution of form into the eternal ether.

Consequences for medicine

On the basis of this spiritual knowledge, the following question appears in its true light: Is it lawful to maintain physical life as long as possible, the life of a premature infant or of a dying person, by means of medical equipment?

"Much could be said about this from the law of God. However, as long as men have their governing laws, a newborn child is already under the influence of these laws. Some laws of the world do not stay within the bounds of what is permissible in the Spirit, i.e., bordering on the spiritual laws, but they often exceed this considerably, thus causing much suffering, hardship, and pain in the souls. No person on earth can imagine the suffering of a soul whose body is connected to intensive care equipment." [16]

From the perspective of matter and of the human laws, physical life must be preserved by all means. But from the spiritual point of view, this often means unimaginable suffering for the souls which are practically tied to their bodies through medical apparatuses. They have to go on living in their bodies, although their lifespan on earth has already run out. For the souls concerned, this very often means a new suffering because these external influences are tied again to their physical bodies. Often, the forced prolongation of their life on earth even results in new, additional soul burdens.

And so, how foolish it is to describe a physician as one who saves lives, when he considers only the physical shell to which he connects apparatuses and dispenses medicines in order to keep the organism alive. What a contradiction it is when, on the one hand, life is preserved by any means and on the other hand abortions are performed.

"Abortion is murder! A person who removes the embryo commits murder, no matter how large it is and in what month of pregnancy the expectant mother is." [17]

From the spiritual point of view, this means that the parents do not assume the responsibility which they have taken upon procreation, namely to give a soul the chance to incarnate and thus expiate a karma. In this respect, they become guilty. Killing an embryo engenders an extremely serious cause which will bring about effects in the present life as well as in the future existences of the reincarnated soul. The reincarnated soul will be led to meet again the person to whom, in a former life on earth, it had not given the chance of incarnation. The person who has burdened himself with this guilt will then expiate a part of the burden of that soul whose incarnation he had once prevented. For in a former incarnation he did not give the possibility of paying off its burden to this soul which, at that particular time, would have reached the adequate maturity to do so, and which is not possible in so short a time in the realm of the souls.

A help for spiritual development

With regard to the situation in the developing countries—it becomes clear from the foregoing that neither birth control, contraception nor development aid on a purely material level represent a lawful and, in the long run, successful solution. Besides the material bread, which it is good to give, people in poor countries need above all the spiritual, living bread: Enlightenment about the law of cause and effect and the spiritual help to liberate themselves from it. Additionally, it is also important that they receive clarification and instruction about fulfilling the law "pray and work," in order to gain spiritual and physical health.

Possibilities of reincarnation in the future

A further reason why the possibilities for incarnation are becoming more and more scarce and the souls are pressing more and more towards incarnation is that the activity of the divine Spirit increases more and more as we enter into the Aquarian Age.

This intensified activity of the primordial power, on the one hand stimulates causes lying in the souls, leading to great catastrophes on a worldwide scale. The consequence of increasing radioactivity and destruction is a decrease in fertility; catastrophes also reduce the possibilities of incarnation. On the other hand, the spiritual striving of people, the urge towards higher spiritual development, is stimulated. Through this reinforced radiation of light power, which transforms all that is base, the vibration of the earth and of its inhabitants will be raised gradually.

Since a soul wanting to incarnate can be attracted only by a mother who has a corresponding vibrational tendency, eventually no low-vibrating, that is, heavily burdened, souls will be able to incarnate in times to come. Instead, more light-filled souls will populate the earth. They will build the Kingdom of the Spirit on earth, which was announced by the prophets of the Old Covenant, by Jesus, the Christ, in the Revelation of John and many other prophecies.

Later on, everything will be transformed to a higher level—the earth and human beings and all Fall-spheres—until finally all has returned to the fine-material spheres of the pure heavens.

We will then live again as pure spirit beings, bright and shining, filled with His Spirit, in His infinite glory of light, in our eternal home, the pure heavens.

References

1. Quotation from H. Bauer "Wiedergeburt - Du warst schon öfter auf dieser Erde - Du wirst wiederkommen!" (Würzburg 1986) p.4 (Reincarnation - You have been on this earth several times - You will come again!).

2. *ob cit.* " p. 4ff.

3. "Gott sprach und spricht durch sie über: Das Leben nach dem Tod. Die Reise deiner Seele" (Würzburg, 1987) p. 61. (God spoke and speaks through her: Life after death. The journey of your soul).

4. Bauer, H. "Wiedergeburt ..." p. 4ff.

5. *cf.* Universelles Leben, publisher: "Wiedergeburt und christlicher Glaube. Du warst schon öfter auf Erden (Würzburg, 1986) p.6ff. (Reincarnation and Christian faith. You have been on earth several times).

6. The anathemas regarding the teaching of reincarnation are quoted in "Reincarnation and Christian faith" p. 9, as well as in H. Bauer, "Reincarnation" p. 89. In the latter, the suppression of the teaching of reincarnation from Christian thought is described extensively (pp. 85-93).

7. *cf.* God spoke ... p. 60.

8. *cf.* "God spoke and speaks through her: The impersonal and the personal God. Who or what is God" (Würzburg, 1986), esp. p. 55ff.

9. *cf.* "God spoke and speaks through her: The Fall of the angels and the return into the Kingdom of God (Würzburg, 1987) pp. 20-45.

10. *ob cit.* pp. 46-93.

11. "Reincarnation and Christian Faith ..." p. 12

12. *cf.:* Universal Life (Publisher): "Your Child and You. A School of Life of Selfless Love. Education of the Infants and Children in Universal Life" (1st Edition Würzburg 1987) p. 95.

13. *cf.* "Reincarnation and Christian Faith ..." p. 16.

14. An impressive example is given in the story "Posthumous Fame" by Manfred Kyber; quoted in "Animal Experiments - Silent Pleas Crying Out to Heaven - Vivisection from a Spiritual Point of View" (Woodbridge, CT, USA, 1996) pp. 34-40.

15. *cf.* "Your Child and You ..." pp. 96ff.

16. *ob cit.* pp. 92ff.

17. *ob. cit.* p. 94.

Appendix

What Is Universal Life

Universal Life can be compared with a great and mighty tree. Its life grew out of a little seed that was planted in the soil of this world: the revelations of the Eternal, of the Christ-of-God, that first took place before a small circle of Christ-friends.

The seed sprouted and became a small seedling that already showed what was hidden within its core: God's light, that is love and wisdom.

As this little seedling grew, it brought further light: the Homebringing Mission of Jesus Christ with the first instructions of the Christ-of-God for a divine life among men.

This work of teaching and explanation that was called into life by the Christ-of-God eighteen years ago quickly grew into a strong plant, a small tree that was rooted in God's love and wisdom: All the basic wisdom of life was given to us men, so that we can find the way into a God-life that brings forth its fruits.

Ever more people drank from the well of divine revelations, and the little tree became a tree of life. People gathered to fulfill the will of God. And so, from the small seed that bore the life, God, grew the great and mighty tree of life called Universal Life, meaning: Living in the Spirit of God, living not only for the individual but for all who are of good will.

The root of this work of God—Christ in His divine revelations given over a period of over 20 years—has reached millions of people, thus fulfilling what Jesus commanded of His own: To bear the gospel of love into all the world. Two thousand years ago Jesus said the following: "When the Spirit of truth comes, he will guide you into all truth." In our time of change, He is come and guides us into all truth—insofar as we can understand His words and receive them into our consciousness.

Now, the fruit of the deed is ripening on the great and mighty crown of the tree of Universal Life. It is the work of God through all those who, attracted by the great light-force of Christ, found their way to those who are building this work of life together. It is a small people, a people in Christ that is emerging for Christ, for a new world under the sign of love and wisdom and of peace, upright men and women who daily live more and more in His Spirit. It is all those who say yes at every moment to the great Spirit of unity, of peace and of love, thus making it possible for the work of the Lord to spread worldwide in few years. It is all those who feel called to put into practice God's love and wisdom in community. Daily, they are active for the higher values of life, for the Kingdom of Peace, the Kingdom of God on this Earth, that was announced already by Jehovah, and for which all Christians pray in the Lord's Prayer.

The Inner Path
"Nearer, My God, to Thee"

"Follow Me" said Jesus of Nazareth. This is a clear challenge which at the same time brings up the question: How can we do this today in the 20th century? The Spirit of the Christ of God teaches the Inner Path in Universal Life, so that we people can find our way to a positive, meaningful life in God. We come to know ourselves, the positive characteristics, but also the human weaknesses. We develop independence, straightforwardness and understanding for our neighbor and overcome frustrations, aggressions, fears and their causes step by step—we practically become our own psychologist. Above all, we experience that we are never alone, but that God is near us and stands by us at all times. With Him, we are able to better master the situations of our life more and more. Through the consistent work on ourselves by mastering our faults and weaknesses with the strength of the Christ of God, the Inner Path leads to a life of love for God and neighbor, to the unity with God.

The Inner Path begins with two courses of preparation. In the first course, we learn to align our feeling, thinking and acting more and more with the Spirit of the Christ of God within us. Then in the second course we become aware of the spiritual power, the divine energies within us, by learning to address the spiritual consciousness centers in the physical body for, among other things, the health of soul and body.

Easy physical exercises to harmonious music support the spiritual alignment of the one who strives for God. They bring about a further balancing of soul and person.

On the first four levels of the Inner Path, the intensive schooling, the student unfolds step by step the first four spiritual levels of evolution—the levels of Order, Will, Wisdom and Earnestness.

On the first level of the inner path of schooling, the level of Order, we learn to put our thoughts in order, to put reins on our speech, to refine our senses, thus turning them within. Here one is called to recognize himself! This means to recognize all human weaknesses, to overcome them with Christ and to no longer do what we have recognized to be negative. Not through fanaticism, but out of love for God, we counter our human ego—our selfishness and our faults. By repenting, forgiving, asking for forgiveness, making amends and not-doing-again, and through the transforming power of Christ, we become free to live in peace with our neighbor—step by step.

On the second level, the level of Will, we become more sensitive and permeable to the spiritual powers. The conscience reacts in a more subtle way. It lets us recognize the various aspects of our humanness about which we knew little or nothing until now. Specific tasks and exercises show this to us little by little. It is thus possible for Christ to let us sense more and more, by way of our sensations, what the will of the Father, the law of God, is. At the same time, we learn true, lawful concentration.

By mastering our human aspects for the most part, we gradually become free from the chains of egocentricity; our spiritual horizon expands; clarity and inner stillness move into us.

We walk the level of Wisdom in order to continue to unfold our spiritual consciousness. The actualization of the eternal laws opens us for the Inner Life ever more, so that we can feel that we are now guided by the Spirit-consciousness, the Inner Helper and Adviser. At the same time, we develop the ability to recognize our neighbors as they are—and not only as they appear to be. This is possible because we have recognized ourselves in the course of this path of schooling of the inner being.

Through the consistent and step-by-step actualization of the eternal laws, we come more and more into the constant fulfillment, into the life of the selfless deed.

On the level of Earnestness, the fruits of fulfilling the divine laws show themselves through a life in the Spirit of God. The spiritually sovereign person who thinks and acts in a clear and straightforward way is mostly free from wanting anything for himself. Completely aligned with the divine, the eternal I Am, he grasps the essential in everything, sees the positive and builds upon it; he recognizes what is lawful and applies it. Thus, the law, God, is able to work through him more and more; he becomes a co-builder of the Kingdom of God on this earth.

When we have unfolded the level of divine Earnestness, we are free from still existing bits of human programs; in this way, we leave the wheel of reincarnation.

Our divine brother, Christ, Himself, then leads us, via our light-filled inner being, to perfection, to the heart of the eternal Father.

The Inner Path can be walked as an intensive course in community with other participants or as a correspondence course using the books of the Inner Path.

Books from the Universal Life Series

This Is My Word
A and Ω
The Gospel of Jesus
The Christ-Revelation
which the world does not know
1078 pages / Order No. S 007en

The Sermon on the Mount
Life in accordance with the law of God
(an excerpt from "This Is My Word")
117 pages / Order No. S 008en

The Great Cosmic Teachings of
JESUS of Nazareth
to His Apostles and Disciples
who could understand them.
With explanations by Gabriele
in the Great Teaching Church
of the Spirit of God - Vol. I
255 pages / Order No. S 317en

Christ Exposes: The Demons' State,
Its Accomplices and Its Victims
88 pages / Order No. S 132en

Liobani: I Tell a Story – Will You Listen?
For parents and children
97 pages, 7 colored illustrations
Order No. S 114en

Your Child and You
102 pages / Order No. S 110en

Live the Moment –
and You Will See and Recognize Yourself
76 pages / Order No. S 315en

Where Did I Come From?
Where Am I Going?
60 pages / Order No. S 407en

God Heals
Healing through the Spirit of God
76 pages / Order No. S 309en

Healing Through the Power of Positive Thinking
55 pages / Order No. S 424en

I Heal You
Three Christ Revelations
80 pages / S 118en

Animal Experiments
Silent Pleas Crying Out to Heaven
48 pages / Order No. S 429en

Gene Manipulation
Man without will, emotionless, controllable
120 pages / Order No. S 502en

The Dangers of Eastern Masters
48 pages / Order No. S 429en

The Inner Path
Courses of preparation

Original Christian Development of Consciousness
for the path within to the divine Self
Reach the spiritual expansion of your consciousness
and become one with God

Course I   Order No. S 122en
Course II   Order No. S 128en

For a free catalog of all our books, cassettes and videos,
please write:

UNIVERSAL LIFE
The Inner Religion
~~PO Box 3549~~
Woodbridge, CT 06525 US
Tel: 1800 846 2691 –USA ~~30-2703~~
eMail: info@universelles-leben.org

Verlag DAS Wort GmbH
im Universellen Leben
Max-Braun-Strasse 2
97828 Marktheidenfeld/Altfeld, Germany
Tel. 9391-504-132 • Fax 9391-504-133